Prologue

Remember late Summer, 2017? Hurricanes made much of the news. I watched it all happen from the safety of my Western Wisconsin living room. Cities from Houston to Tampa to San Juan get battered and flooded. And the news footage had a pattern. First, shoppers emptied grocery and hardware stores. Then store windows got covered in plywood sheets. Then reporters stood by the town levies until the wind and rain forced them into shelters. The following days of footage included sad images of flooding, and of people stranded on roofs.

We don't to worry about that up here in the land of cheese, lakes and beer. Blizzards, deep freezes and thunderstorms are our weather concerns, so hurricane survival is an abstract idea. Still, I wondered what my family would do if we had a few days' notice of a major flood event. Seeing coverage of plywood on boarded windows gave me an idea. I've been building boats out of cheap plywood for years. If the boat only needs to last a few days or few hours, if it must be built with easy-to-obtain materials; what techniques could get you a use? How inexpensive could it be? Boat building isn't difficult, so, my thought experiment turned into a challenge.

The result: It *is* possible to build a boat in three days, for under $50, using basic tools and materials. That's what this book is about. Are you ready to give it a try? Let's walk through this process together.

Contents

Boat Building is Easy

Boat building sounds intimidating until you think about it. Fresh water weighs 64 pounds per cubic foot. Give or take. That means four cubic feet of water weighs 256 pounds. And any object that takes up four cubic feet of space, and weighs 256 pounds or less, can float. Imagine building an empty wooden box one foot tall, two feet wide and two feet long. Maybe the wood weighs 20 pounds. Put the box in water. If you stand on it, and if you weigh less than 236 pounds (256 points minus the weight of the wood), you will stay just above water.

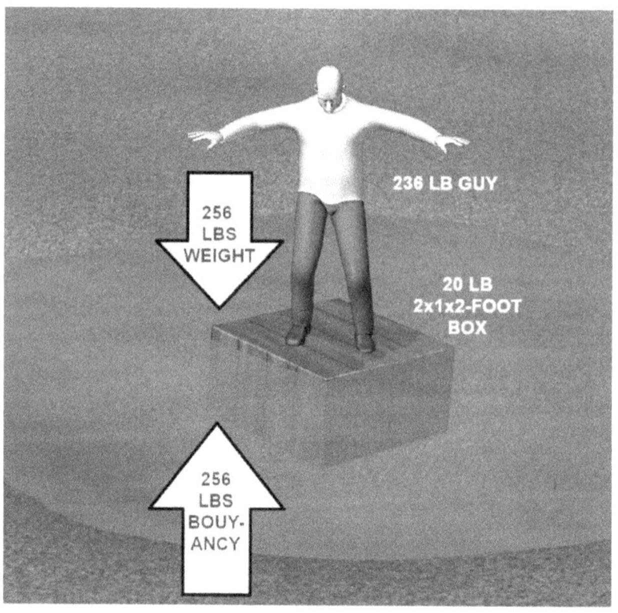

Well, good luck balancing on a two-by-two box in the water. That box isn't so much of a boat as it is … flotsam. Isn't 'flotsam' that a fun word? We want our boat to be more than something to cling on to for dear life. So stability matters. Instead of building a one-foot tall box, picture building a box that is six inches tall, two feet wide and four feet long. The shape still takes up four cubic feet of space, only now it is spread out along the surface of the water. That makes it harder to tip; you could probably stand on it comfortably.

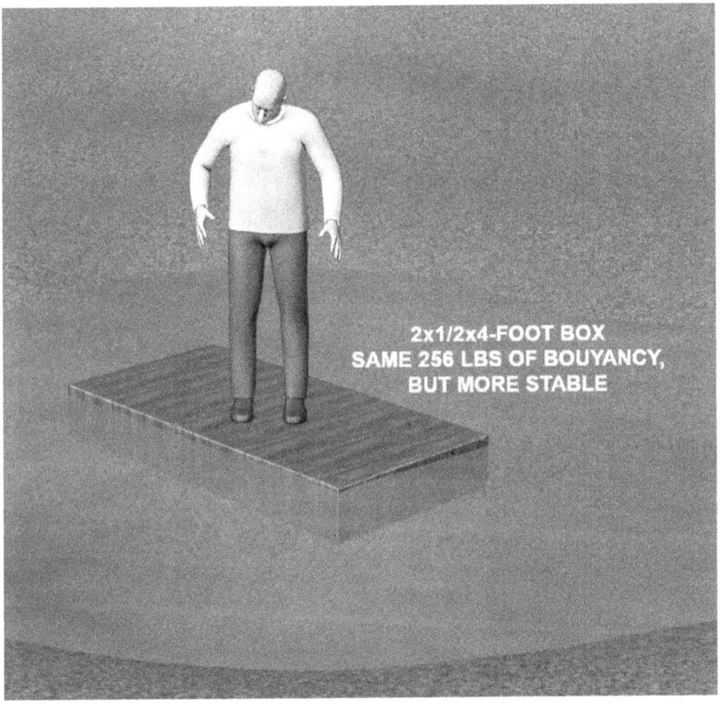

Congratulations! You have just hypothetically created the world's ugliest paddle board.

My point is, if you can build a box, you can build a boat. Boat building can be expensive and fancy. I've seen beautiful watercraft built with years of expert carpentry. Good for those boat builders. I'm not one of them. For our purposes, a boat must be stable enough not to dump you out, must be buoyant enough to keep you above water, and must be water-tight enough not to sink too fast. The rest is optional.

Tools

When you look through this list of tools, notice how no tool is specifically for boat building. Chances are, you own most of them already. Being a homeowner, and many people up here in Wisconsin are, requires a basic tool collection. If you don't, my guess is that the tools you don't own are clamps and a jigsaw. Normally you'll find these among woodworking geeks, like me. Obtain a jigsaw and some clamps is a good idea regardless. Imagine a dining room chair breaks. You can fix it with a clamp and some wood glue. Likewise, your jigsaw can help you cut out that broken PVC pipe in the laundry room. Not only will this more than make up for the cost of the tools, you can brag to your loved ones about how handy you are.

Feel like doing this build for under $50, still. Consider this tool list your first challenge. You can spend well more than 50 dollars on tools alone, not to mention parts. My boat was closer to $35, because I already had some of these tools lying around. If I'm perfectly honest with you, there was some begging and smidge of dumpster diving, too. All part of the fun.

One more note, here: I am listing these tools in order of importance. In my opinion.

Jigsaw

Price: $10-20.

Use: The jigsaw is a hand saw with a little oscillating blade that allows you to cut wood, especially plywood, into curved and strait edges.

Tip: Cutting lines takes practice. Build something small before building a boat. Make a decoration. Build a doll house for the kids. Understand that jigsaws have different blades for different cuts and different materials. A standard wood blade works fine. We're not cutting tight curves, so a blade for strait cuts is all we need. Do read the safety instructions that come with a jigsaw. Use common sense when using one. Please do not cut off your thumb.

Treat yourself: I've found paying extra for a cordless jigsaw is worth it. A cordless jigsaw might be less powerful than a corded one at the same price point. That matters little when cutting ¼-inch plywood and 1x4 pine, which is all we need it for here. The freedom of cordless-ness is worth it. Some jigsaws come with fancy lights that illuminate what you are cutting. Some come with blowers that blow away saw dust. Of the many extra features possible, cordless-ness is my favorite.

Alternative: Hand saw. These are cheaper, slower and probably safer. They work fine if you have the time and want to build your forearm muscles.

Power Drill

Price: $10-20

Use: Put the boat together. You'll use about 100 screws, so a power drill saves substantial time.

Treat yourself: With drills, you get what you pay for. For attaching ¼-inch plywood to anything, an inexpensive cordless drill works fine. Like with jigsaws, cordless are more convenient with less power, unless you are willing to pay more.

Accessories: Get a #2 Phillips head, and at least one smaller head. We'll be using #2 Phillips screws and a smaller kind of wood screw. You'll also need a ¼-inch drill bit.

Tip: Buy cordless power drills and jigsaws from the same company. They'll likely have interchangeable batteries. Jigsaws and screwdrivers are seldom used together; either you are cutting or screwing. If your power drill battery dies, you can use your jigsaw battery as a backup.

Alternative: Hand drill. They work great. I use them for big, heavy projects like backyard sheds. Hand drills need no recharging, have plenty of torque and work fast. The drawbacks? They require pilot holes and are difficult to use in tight spots.

Safety goggles

Price: $2-10

Use: Wear them. Do not build a boat or do any woodworking without safety goggles. Eyes are 80% of our sensory input. Don't wreck your eyes.

Treat yourself: High-end safety goggles are more comfortable, have less glare and are less likely to fog up during use.

Alternatives: None. Regular eyeglasses offer limited protection and welding masks are impractical.

Earmuffs

Price: $2-10

Use: Wear them. Hearing is fragile, and when it's gone, it's gone for good. Don't consider that medical advice. I'm no doctor. Health notwithstanding, earmuffs are comfortable. What's more annoying than a screaming power tool? I cut and drill better when my head isn't rattling. Earmuffs also eliminate distractions. And requests from spouses: "Sorry, honey. I was wearing earmuffs!"

Tip: Earmuffs are an absolute must for your kids when they are around.

Alternatives: Ear plugs work just as well. They are disposable. If you forget to buy enough, like I would, you'll have to make an unexpected run to the hardware store.

Pencils

Price: $1-3
Use: Essential tool for drawing your cuts and making plans. In theory, you can make a boat without using any symmetry or measurements. … That sounds fun, in fact.
Treat yourself: Mechanical pencils aren't much more expensive, are more precise, and require no sharpening. I use mechanical pencils.
Alternative: Pencils produce thin lines that are erasable. Chalk is erasable, but makes wide, inaccurate lines. Pens and knives make thin and accurate lines that cannot be erased.

Tape measure

Price: $5-$10
Use: Measuring things that are long. Tape measures also tell you when your boat is too big to fit inside your vehicle.
Tip: Ten feet is enough. If you don't already own one, your neighbor almost certainly does. Ask permission before borrowing it from their garage. Burglary is a felony.

Ruler

Price: $1-$10

Use: Draw straight lines in small places. Measure anything less than a foot. Expect to get a lot of use out of this tool. If you aren't using it, chances are you put it somewhere, can't find it. Well, if you look harder, you'll see it's in front of your face.

Tip: Buy a few dozen and scatter them around the workshop. That way you're guaranteed to find one when you need one.

Tip: Just kidding?

Treat yourself: I enjoy my fancy ruler with a compass and 90-degree edge thing, especially when drawing cuts for beams on 1 x 4 pine.

Carpenter's Square

Price: $10-$15

Use: Draw right angles for lofting. 'Lofting' is boat builder talk for drawing layouts from plans onto the actual wood. Draw and measure strait lines between 1 and 2 feet. Obtain right angles. This is another tool that has many non-boat uses around the house.

Tip: You'll use this more than you expect.

Alternative: Other stuff makes 90-degree angles. You could use a sheet of poster board or square of plywood, or a large book. These alternatives are not as accurate.

Strait Edge

Price: $5-$20
Use: A strait edge can be a strait piece of high-quality wood or metal, or a 4-foot purpose-built aluminum beam with a level. Use these to draw lines for cutting strips of plywood and for measuring connection points along the bottom of the boat. Strait edges are handy for general home projects like drywall replacement.
Tip: If the edge isn't touching the surface that you are drawing on, don't trust your hand to keep the strait line going. Make sure all parts of the strait edge touch the surface that you are marking. If needed, weigh down or clamp things tight.

Clamps

Price: $20-30
Use: Holding the parts of the boat in place while you fasten or draw on things.
Tip: Get at least one 3-foot clamp and 2 or 3-foot-long clamps. The 2-3-inch pinch - y things are always handy to have around, as well.
Alternative: None. You could concoct an ingenious rig made of bricks and rubber bands, or whatever else is lying around the house. It's easier to buy or borrow clamps.

Scissors

Price: $1-2
Use: These are handy for cutting poster board. I use poster board mostly for drawing stencils. Other applications include fabric (Are you crazy enough to put a sail on this? Good for you!), cushioning, and anything else too delicate for a jigsaw.
Treat yourself: Wander into a craft store and you can find specialty scissors.
Alternatives: None.

Rubber or latex gloves

Price: $1-2
Use: Applying Epoxy to the wood. Epoxy is harmful on skin.
Tip: Find something reasonably thick within the price range. Rough wood and splinters can tear gloves. Small amounts of skin contact on Epoxy is, in my opinion as a non-doctor, more of a nuisance then a health threat.
Treat yourself: If your friends ask what the gloves are for, consider how often rubber gloves appear in horror, crime and medical dramas. Pick a disturbing, yet plausible reason you own so many rubber gloves.
Alternatives: None.

Materials

Plywood

Price: $25-$40
Type: ¼- inch thickness. Go cheap. You do not need Marine Grade for this. DO use plywood. Particle board or wafer board are no substitute.
Quantity: Two 8 by 4-foot sheets
Use: Determines the shape of the boat. Helps keep water out. Provides structural support.
Tip: Plywood is an amazing material. It is inexpensive. The scraps are non-toxic. It is strong and flexible while being easy to work with. Front-line aircraft were made of plywood as late as World War Two.
Alternatives: Many. You could use oak strips, aluminum, fiberglass, even iron or concrete. I once built a kayak out of duct tape. This book is about plywood kayaks, because plywood is the easiest material to use (I think). If this boat build is easy and fun, go nuts and build a boat out of a weirder material.

1 by 2 corded wood

Price: $5
Type: 1 by 2-inch, Pine or Cedar. Cheaper furring strips are acceptable. Cedar is more expensive, but it smells nice.
Quantity: Two 8-foot lengths
Use: Structural strength and shaping. The keel (bottom), stem and stern (tips) and cockpit use these.
Alternatives: Metal is a stronger and more expensive alternative. It requires different tools and techniques than the ones described in this book. PVC pipe is a cheaper, weaker alternative. I've built a boat using PVC pipe … you get what you pay for.

Screws

Price: $5
Type: 1-inch Phillips wood screws
Quantity: 100 or so
Use: Attaching wood parts
Tip: Basic construction screws work fine.
Alternatives: None. Nails are not an alternative. The boat is fragile until assembly is complete. One wrong hammer swing, and you get a big hole in the plywood. Also, nails have less grip, so more glue is needed.

Epoxy

Price: $15
Type: The five minute or hour stuff works.
Quantity: 16-20oz
Use: Seal all seams and screw heads.
Tip: Epoxy keeps the water out. It is toxic and unpleasant to work with. Use protective gloves. Use in a well-ventilated space. Read all the instructions and warnings. I'll go into details about Epoxy later.
Alternatives: You could use cheaper water-tight construction adhesive. I only trust Epoxy for continuous (two hours or longer) underwater emersion. If you have chemical allergies and must use an alternative to Epoxy, pay attention to whether that adhesive is "water resistant", "watertight" or "waterproof". These terms mean different things. If the instructions say the product isn't intended for long-term submersion, believe it. Also, most alternatives required more product. 20oz of tar, for example, won't seal-in as much as 20oz of Epoxy.

Urethane

Price: $5
Type: Spray on or manual application.
Quantity: 6-12 oz is enough.
Use: Make the wood water resistant.
Tip: Get a layer of urethane over every surface. It extends the amount of time the wood can be wet. Since I build lots of boats, I prefer spray-on. It's less product per cost, but you don't have to put on rubber gloves and risk touching the stuff. Urethane hands are not fun, and the stuff is difficult to remove from you skin.
Alternatives: There must be alternatives. I'm no expert. Every home improvement store has a selection of wood finish that includes waxes, resins and other covering. Look into that and get back to me.

Painter's tape

Price: $3
Type: The cheap stuff is fine.
Quantity: Less than a role. Perhaps 24 feet.
Use: Keeps the Epoxy from leaking before it hardens.
Alternatives: Any non-plastic tape. Masking tape, various gauzes also work. Duct tape or packing tape won't do, because we'll want to paint over this part.

Paint

Price: $10.
Type: Latex. We are covering it in urethane, so don't worry about expensive Marine Grade paint. Dark color is best.
Quantity: A quart or less.
Use: Covers the blotches of Epoxy and painter's tape along the bottom of the boat.
Tip: You could sand-away the painter's tape and Epoxy lumps. That takes extra time and requires an extra tool. I say, be fast, be sloppy and hide your mess.
Alternatives: If looks aren't a factor, you don't need paint.

A closet rod or pipe

Price: $2-$10, though chances are you can find one dirt cheap at an estate sale or store closing.
Type: Whatever you can use for the paddle. Six feet should be long enough.
Quantity: 1
Use: Paddling
Tip: Wooden closet rods are about $10, but any equivalent shape would work. You can use a 2x2 length of pine and sand or jigsaw the edges into a rod. PVC piping, if stiff enough, is an option.

Something to sit on

Price: $2-$5
Type: A few 2x4s or some spare plywood. An unused pillow or blanket for padding.
Quantity: Enough to sit on and distribute your weight.
Use: Distributes your weight over the plywood. Adds some comfort.
Tip: You don't want your weight focused on a few square inches of the bottom. This could crack the plywood or open a seam.

Life jacket

Price: $20-$30
Type: Look up what is recommended for your age and body type
Use: Prevents you from dying.
Tip: Consider this the most important part of your kayak once it is completed. If the kayak sinks, the worst that happens is you lose some money and need to (get to) build another kayak. In theory, you could just float along a lake with your life jacket and a fishing rod in hand.
Treat yourself: I like to put carabiners on my life jackets to hold cameras, car keys and other items. If you are going somewhere remote, attach an emergency radio.

One final word about tools and materials. You won't need everything right away. If time is no factor, space your purchases out. That way, when life events prevent you from completing this, or if you decide that boat building is for losers, you're not stuck with things you'll never use. Here is the 'order of appearance' of parts and materials so you can plan accordingly.

Stage	Tool	Material
Layout and first cuts	Earmuffs, Goggles, Pencil, Straight Edge, Carpenter's Square, Ruler	Plywood
Cutting the bottom and attaching the sides	Clamps, Power drill, Tape measure	1x2 Corded Wood Screws
Adding the top cover	Scissors	
Waterproofing	Rubber gloves	Painter's tape, Epoxy, Urethane
Finishing touches		Paint, Closet rod, Something to sit on, Life jacket

And that's that. Let's start building.

The Part Where We Build It

The first cut turns a single 8'x4' plywood sheet into two 8'x2' sheets. Pretty easy. The trick is first to draw a line through the center of the sheet. For this, I use the carpenter's square. From the edge of the sheet, measure and mark the 2' point. Repeat every two feet or so along the 8' length of the sheet. You'll see what I mean in a moment.

Depending on the quality of the sheet, this might or might not be the center of it. Maybe the 8'x4' sheet is actually 8'x4' 1/3". That's OK. The goal is to find the center line. To compensate, measure and mark out 2' from both sides of the plywood. Find and mark the center point of the two marks. Using a straight edge or a cord of wood, draw a line connecting those marks.

Let's walk through this. Here is a diagram. The thick gray lines show the pencil marks we're about to make:

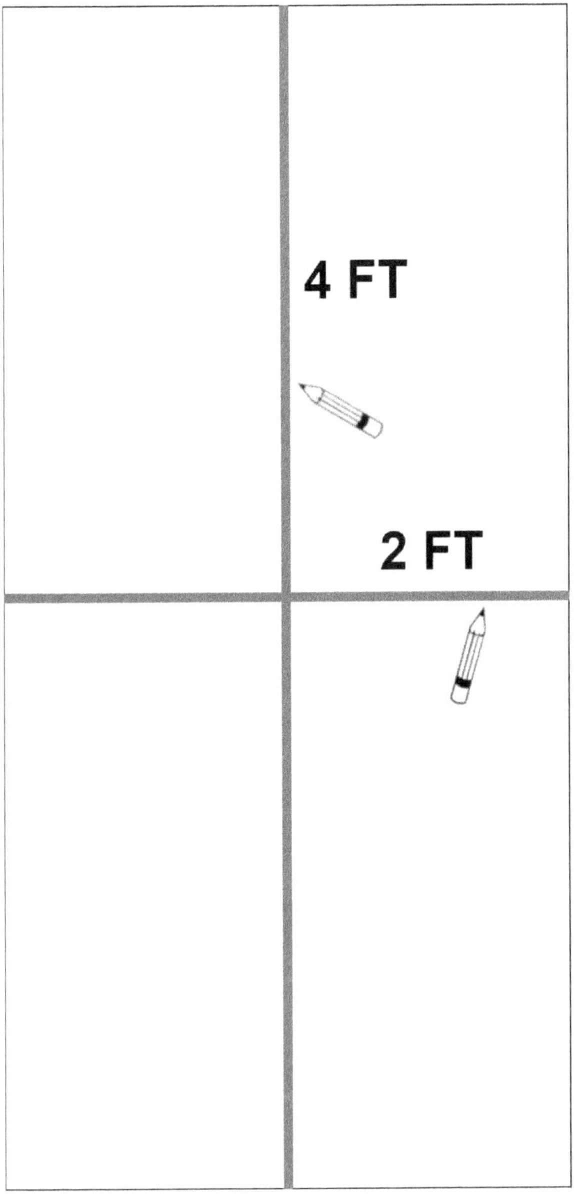

4 FT
2 FT

The carpenter's square helps us find the longitudinal (long-ways) center of the sheet. I'm using a long level, too. A strait piece of wood works about as well.

So, let's trace away …

Are the lines strait and clear? I like to step back and eyeball such things from a distance. If it looks good, it is time for the first cut. With the magical power of the jigsaw, the 4'x8' sheet of plywood becomes two 2'x8' sheets. You could use a hand saw for this step. It would save money and provide an excellent workout. I'm not that ambitious.

Now for the cutting. Jigsaw work takes practice, as it involves muscle memory. If your cuts are 'wobbly' within an eight of an inch, you are in good shape. Imperfections will not be noticable and the glue will fill in the gaps.

Now, take one of the 8′x2′s and turn it into the bottom of the kayak. The first step is to draw a cross that separates it into four 4′x1′ sections. We won't cut this cross; but use it to help us draw the rounded-out profile of the bottom.

Here are the marks we'll make. Don't worry about the curvy lines yet, though:

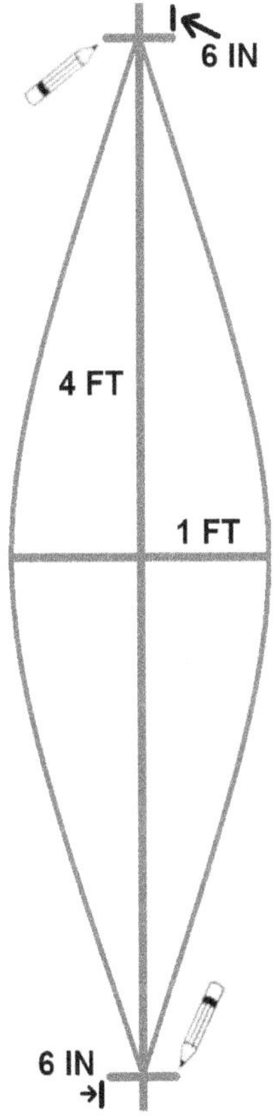

This bottom could be two feet wide at its widest, and up to 8 feet long. The bigger the bottom, the more stable the boat. The drawback? Each side panel sheet would have to be longer than 8 feet, as these must wrap around the curve of the bottom. Our plywood is only 8 feet long, so we'd have to glue extra panels. The fewer items we glue, the fewer opportunities water has to enter the boat.

I'd rather have each side be a single sheet with no cuts. The bottom needs to be shorter than 8 feet and thinner than two feet to make that happen. We'll want the top of the sides to be longer than the bottom of the sides, which requires an even smaller bottom. You'll see what I mean soon. So, let's mark six inches in on each long end. Why six inches? Guestimation. The end result is that we create a 7'x2' bottom.

Using the carpenter's square and a straight edge, draw the lines on the plywood, then Mark the 6-inch points and draw the longitudinal line.

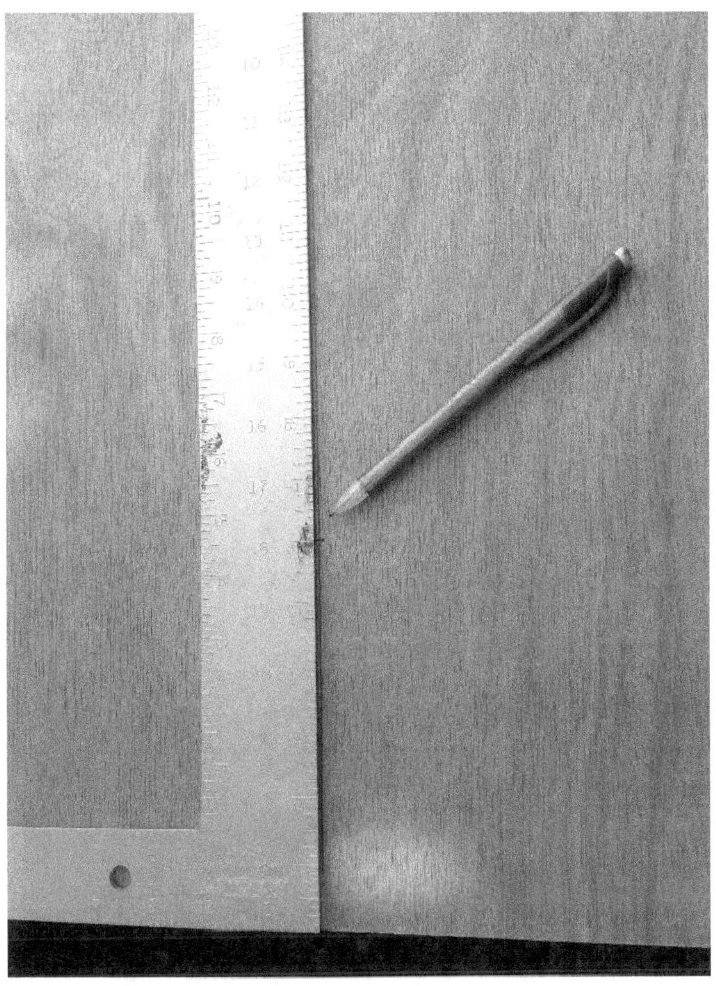

Notice the carpenter's square and straight edge work at this stage. The square sets the 90-degree angle with all the precision we need, which isn't a terrible amount, and the edge helps us trace out the parts of the line that are beyond the square's reach.

How do we make those curves? Well, this part is kind of fun. Clamp down any long, bendy scrap of wood, making sure the marks are hit. Then trace. Here I used a thin strip of plywood.

Then repeat on the other side …

Then cut.

I find working outside in the yard more enjoyable
than in the garage. It's a way to get some time in the
sun. The outdoors provides the best possible
ventilation. And the grass takes care of any
shavings and sawdust.

I went inside to keep cutting when it started raining. I've never jig-sawed in the rain, though, so I guess do what you prefer. Pardon my messy garage.

Here is our result. It is the first indication that this thing we are building might be a boat.

Before we move on to the next step, let's take a moment and cut out the sides of the kayak. Using the other 8'x2' panel, find the long-ways center line, and cut out two 8'x1' panels.

And cut. My cordless jigsaw battery was running low, so I used my corded jigsaw here.

Progress is coming along nicely. We've got two sides and bottom. How will we connect them? The answer is to use a bunch of little blocks. Cut some 1'x2' length of wood every inch until we have thirty or so.

Now, I have a confession to make here. It is possible to cut these out using a jigsaw. They don't have to be perfectly accurate. But I have a fine chop saw that saved fifteen minutes of time. A chop saw is not on the tools list. If you do woodworking in general, I recommend getting one.

These will be connectors and mostly hidden, so if you are short on time, don't fuss too much over exact measurements. If each block can hold two screws, you're in good shape. You'll see what I mean shortly.

We will put these blocks along the bottom edge of
the boat, every 6 inches. To mark every six inches, I
created a marky-thing that marks by scratcing screw
tips onto the plywood surface. This tool is quite
handy for all its simpliticty. I've used it for building
fancier sailboats, as well as duct tape canoes.

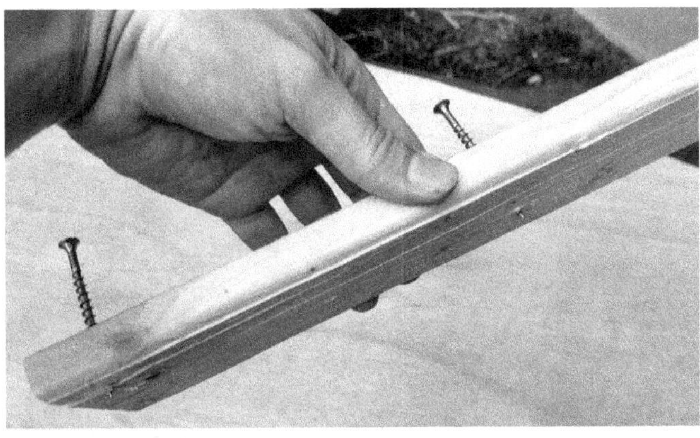

The blocks get screwed on like so. Be careful – do drill pilot holes. Even then, some might crack. They are easy to make, so be ready to make more. You might wonder why no angle has been cut into the side of each cube; the sides will not connect with the bottom at a 90-degree angle (this is called a 'chine' in boat language). The reason is, I didn't know what that angle would be beforehand. And plywood is flexible enough for those few degrees not to matter.

A few of them did crack while I was drilling, so I made extra.

The next step will be to attach the sides, which means we'll put another screw into each block, from a different angle. Avoid that by adding each screw slightly away from the center of each block.

Here is what the blocks look like when added. Note that the tips (stem and stern) have no blocks. This is to leave room for the stem and sternposts.

Now we have set up a way to connect the sides and bottom, let's make sure they align. Take one of the sides and align it with the bottom.

You can prop the side next to the bottom with bricks, books or claps. The plywood is flexible enough for that at this scale. We'll want the overlapping sides at the front and back to be equal.

Use a ruler to determine how far each end overlaps
the tip of the bottom. Adjust the side until both ends
have the same overlap. In this case, it is just under 4
inches. Mark this point.

Enter the carpenter's square again. Our goal is to make each side panel a trapezoid, where the top is longer than the bottom. This trapezoid will, you'll see, add boat-y curves to our kayak. To outline it, place the corner of the carpenter's square along the mark at the overlap point. Put the edge of the square at the opposite corner of the plywood sheet. Trace the line. Repeat for the other end.

This is the shape we need (Again, pardon the messy garage – it started raining again). It's time to repeat this process for the other side of the boat.

And this is the outcome:

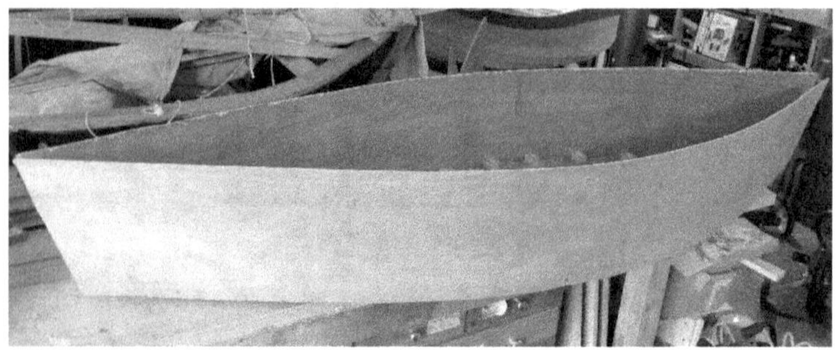

Well, I'm getting excited now. Are you?

Attach the sides to the bottom with screws, one screw per block. You may need to hold the top tips together with a clamp. Again, make sure to put the screw away from the center of each block, as colliding screws will cause the block to crack. You may want to drill pilot holes, depending on the quality of the wood.

That complete, we enter the toughest phase of the build, so I'll pace myself. Think of the boat as a big wooden taco. Or pita pocket. To float well and fit us comfortably, we need to make opening as wide as it can be, without cracking the shell. Fortunately, plywood is stronger and more flexible than taco shells.

Start by taking the 1x2 and cutting two, 2-foot lengths. One will go toward the stem (front), one will go toward the stern (back). As to how far forward or rearward, let's figure out where our butt will sit. For simplicity, I'm placing my butt just 'rear' of the center of the boat's bottom. This means, the cockpit opening will be in the center of the boat; as far from the front as it is from the back.

Making sense?

To start, let's use our tape measure to find the middle of the top edge of each side. Once found and marked, we're going to take those 1x2's we just cut, place them to widen our big wooden 'taco shell'.

Where do we place them? I guessed 18 inches in front of, and 18 inches behind the middle of the boat. Use the carpenter's square to measure and mark these points, then carefully insert the 1x2's. Listen for cracking noises. If two feet is too wide for the 'taco', cut the 1x2's down a few inches.

It's not the end of the world if it cracks. Worst case scenario, you need to rebuild one of the sides, and you already have practice building these. A small crack is more likely and will only affect the boat's curvature a little. Hey, we're not perfectionists! If we were, we'd still be making measurments on our more expensive, marine-grade plywood sheets.

Line up the carpenter's square lined up along the top-center point. Then measure and mark 18 inches forward, and 18 inches rearward. In the picture on the next page I put in some 1x2's to open the sides a little.

Be mindful of this gap, because this area is where we will put our bodies. If too big, we invite water in from the top. Too small, and we can't fit inside.

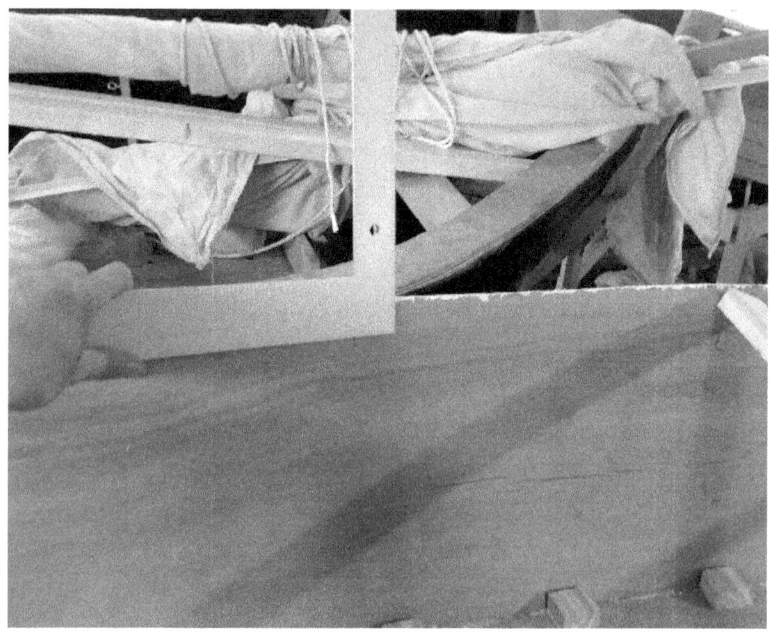

Now both 1x2's are in. If you are satisfied, screw them to the side panels. Make sure the top, wider edge is lined up flat. There will be a little gap where the 1x2 meets the side, since these don't meet at a 90-degree angle. That's OK.

Next, we cut another two sections of 1x2's and place each along the seams at the stem and stern. You could either measure the stem and stern ahead of time, or you could cut a rough length and chop off the overlap with a jigsaw afterwards. I did the later.

Here they are, cut down to the sides. Attach with screws every six inches or so.

OK. This is looking more and more like a boat every step. Let's flip it over and begin waterproofing.

We will make this waterproof with Epoxy. Epoxy is a glue that starts liquid and turns solid. Keep in mind that our craftsmanship isn't perfect. If we tried to glue the sides together as they are now, much of the Epoxy would leak through before it dries. That happened to me once. It formed a near-indestructible blob on the garage floor, and my wife almost killed me. Let's not let that happen. We'll place painter's tape along the seams to catch any wet Epoxy before it can escape.

I had leftover drywall gauze and decided to use it. Was it necessary? I don't know, but it couldn't hurt. The goal is to cover a good 2-3 inches of area around each seam; however, you make that happen.

I covered the gauze in tape. This should do the trick.

Flip the boat back over. It is time to start gluing! If you haven't used Epoxy before, practice gluing some scrap wood before committing it to your boat.

UNDERSTAND BEFORE YOU GLUE

- Epoxy is toxic to the skin and lungs. Maybe other body parts, too. Wear rubber or latex gloves. Glue in a well-ventilated room.
- Epoxy stinks. Get permission from your roommates and loved ones before inflicting such stench into their lives.
- If Epoxy had eyes, it would be glaring at you with evil intent.
- Epoxy is *the* adhesive for wooden boat building. I've tried alternatives. Nothing beats its strength and water repellence.

We're on the same page about what we're dealing with, so let's talk about basic usage.

Again, you'll want to practice on some scrap wood before using it on the boat. The adhesive comes in two tubes: one for the hardener, and one for the resin. The resin gives the glue mass, so it can fill cracks. The hardener reacts with the resin to create a bond as strong as super glue while contributing to the mass.

Mix these in 1-1 proportions. Don't mix too much at the same time. Find a spot on the bottom of your boat near a seam and squeeze a quarter-size puddle of each. You can place one puddle one on top of the other or place them side by side. Stir with a stick. Sometimes the package contains a plastic stirring straw. When they mix, the chemical reaction creates heat. This isn't noticeable below 1oz. It is when you mix two 3.5oz packets … it gets hot.

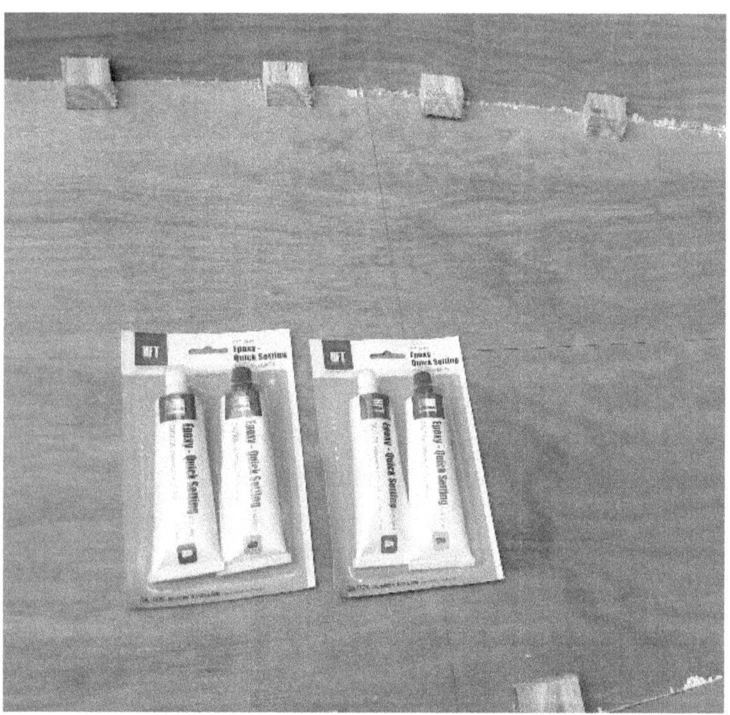

By the way, DO NOT MIX EPOXY WITH YOUR UPROTECTED FINGER. Have I mentioned Epoxy is harmful to skin? You'll know the mix is complete when the clear resin and hardener turn cloudy, depending on the brand and instructions.

When mixed, take a piece of scrap wood and swoop the glob to the gap between the side of the boat and the bottom. The tape we place should prevent the glue from leaking through. Use your gloved fingers to fill the crack along the seam. Coat an inch or so out from the crack in both directions.

Make more puddles as needed, until the inner seam is covered. Get the stem and stern, too. Basically, any gap where one piece of wood touches another needs Epoxy covering it. Do not worry about covering flat areas, like the sides and bottom of the boat. We'll coat those in cheaper Urethane.

That painter's tape along the middle of the side in the following picture, by the way, is for painting later. The glue will make blobs. These blobs could be sanded down; it's faster to hide them under dark paint. Over the years I have learned that dark paint hides a lot of sloppy work. Expedience is the game here, though.

When the inside of the boat is glued, wait 24 hours for the adhesive to fully cure. Then we can flip the boat over and tackle the outer parts.

In the meantime, let's complete some side-tasks. An important yet easy task is creating the keel. The keel is the 'spine' of the boat. It absorbs the weight of the paddler and other forces that pull on the boat from multiple directions. You can also think of a keel like the keystone in an arch. For this reason, traditional boat building starts with the keel.

The keel is a 1x2 length of pine. Take your upright boat. Measure a few inches in from the bottom of the stem, and an equal amount from the stern. If the front and back tip of your boat is 6 feet, the keel should be about 5 feet, 8 inches. Cut out the keel from the 1 by 2, then cut a triangle into the tips of the keel for streamlining.

Does it look like this? Good.

Place the boat on top of the keel. Center the keel along the center of the boat. The boat is upright, and you are looking down on it. Find a spot on the 'floor' of the boat that is a few inches from the stern. Screw a one-inch-long screw to connect the bottom to the keel. The screw should be short enough not to poke through the bottom of the keel. If it does, you can Dremel off the part that sticks out, or find a shorter screw.

Not too hard, right? If your keel doesn't align, try again. We can always fill the holes in with Epoxy.

Wood bends. For a thin 1x2, you won't need to wet it down. Bend the far tip to the stem, then repeat what you just did with the stern. If it looks like the next picture, we're in good shape.

From here, place a screw every six inches along the centerline of the bottom. Here the measuring tool with the two screws in the wood six inches apart is again handy. That should hold it in place. Cover each screw head with a smear of Epoxy. Do the same in the seam where the keel meets the bottom.

Another thing we can do while the Epoxy is curing, is create the cockpit. Is this necessary? What we've built already looks like a canoe, and canoes are handy watercraft already. Well, there are two reasons to make a cockpit. First, the gunnels, that's the top of the sides, are flimsy. They are only a quarter-inch thick and could crack if you have grip them the wrong way. One we'll need to strengthen them. In the past, I've reinforced gunnels with strips of overlapping quarter-inch plywood.

That could work here, except for the second reason; a boat this small can easily get swamped. Picture fishing on a calm lake, and some jackass water skis in front of you (Yes, this has happened to me). An open boat is more likely to be swamped than one with a cover over it. This cover isn't perfectly sealed. We are making a wide cockpit. But having a covered stem and stern is at least enough of a seal to slow the onrush of water in time for you to react.

OK, I'm going to call out a third reason. A top cover is a nice platform to hold your beverages and fishing gear.

Remember that second sheet of plywood? Let's begin this part by putting that sheet on top of the boat.

That looks like an interesting art project from this angle.

Trace the sheet where it meets the edges of the tops (the "gunnels", in Pirate Speak). You'll have a teardrop shape. Cut that shape out, place it over the boat, and this is what you get:

There is something I find deeply gratifying about that tracing step. I don't know why.

If you Epoxy this sheet to the top, there is no way this boat could swamp. But where would you sit? Here is where the poster board comes into play. We're going to create a stencil to cut out the cockpit.

From the middle of the boat, measure and mark 3 inches in from each side, at the midpoint of the boat. Cut a curve out of a corner of your poster board. Align it to the 3-inch mark. Trace that curve. Flip the paper over. Repeat this process until you have drawn an oval on the top center of the boat.

How long does this oval have to be? I guessed 2-3 feet. It depends on your body and your flexibility.

With the oval drawn, we'll need to drill a hole big enough to fit the jigsaw blade. This is done with the ¼" drill bit. Put the hole near the line. Do it INSIDE the oval, not on the outside of it. I have made that mistake before. Cut away.

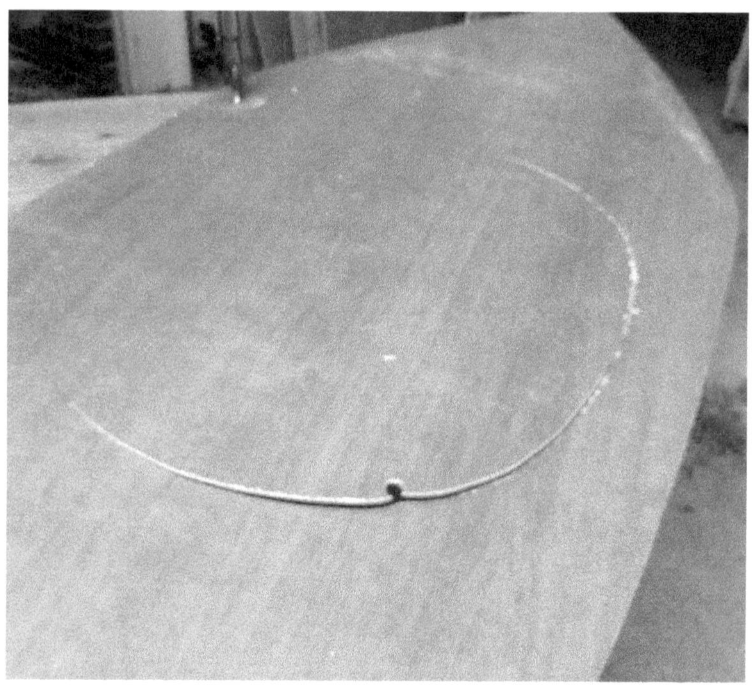

See the result on the next page. I think my body could fit through that. If you have doubts about yours, carefully put your body through it. Keep in mind that this plywood, cut this way, is fragile. Note that most kayaks have the cockpit toward the back. I didn't do that, for simplicity sake.

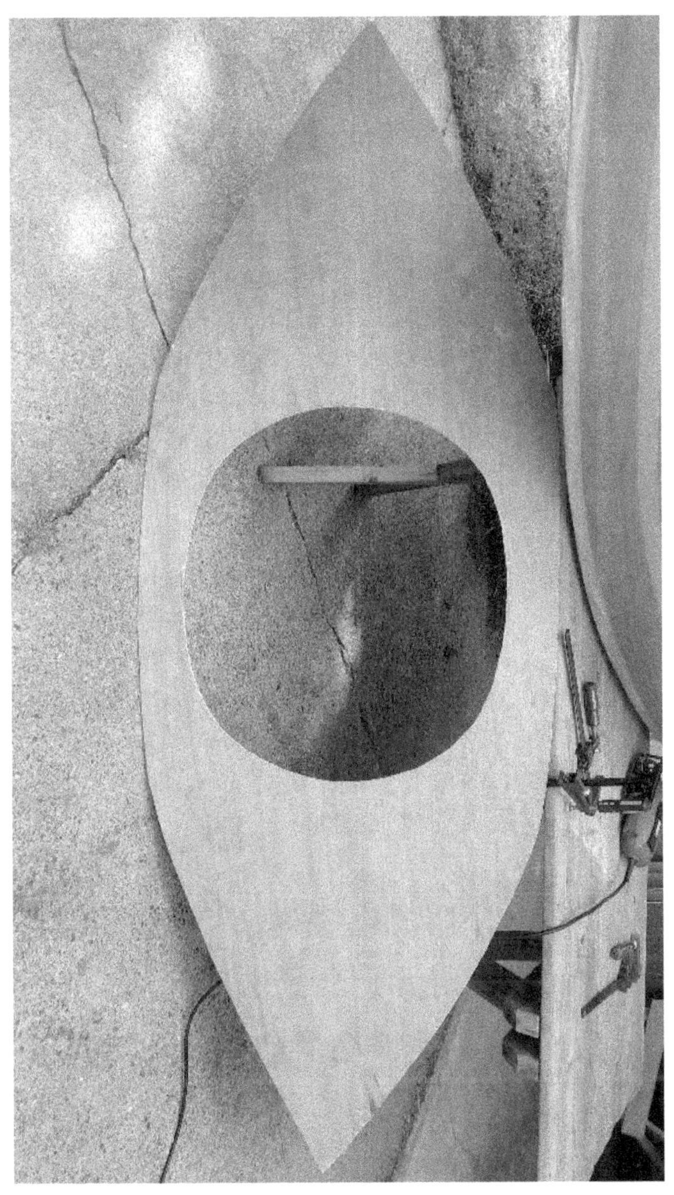

As fun as making the top cover was, we have more
Epoxy to add. The Epoxy on the inner part of the
boat should be hard enough now to permit us to flip
the boat over. This time we will cover the outside,
specifically, the seam of the keel and the tape
around the bottom edge. Spread glue along the
seams of the keel, too.

Leave the boat upside down and wait for this glue to dry. Note that curing and drying are different things. Glue can be dry enough to paint on, but if you move parts around before it is cured (fully hardened), then cracks form and the bond is weaker.

When dry enough, let's paint. Like I said earlier, dark colors hide sloppy craftsmanship. This part will be underwater, anyway. What matters is that it is the only part that is under water.
I'm painting over the tape, which is covered in Epoxy, anyway. It is tempting to sand the glued area so the paint has a rough texture that it can grip. The latex paint gripped fine here without sanding.

When the paint is dry, let's attach the cover. I ran a smaller line of epoxy with my fingers along the inner seams. I also screwed the cover to the 1x2's along the cockpit front and rear. If you have leftover blocks, it is a good idea to use these to help keep the cover in place, like how we attached the bottom to the sides. Here, it doesn't matter as much. A bad seal won't skin the boat, and the structure is already quite strong.

This is also the part where I sprayed urethane over every surface. Urethane is less toxic, less fowl-smelling, less 'evil' than Epoxy. But do follow similar safety guidelines.

- Keep it off your skin. Wash it off with paint thinner, rubbing alcohol and similar chemicals. Follow that up with water and soap. Water and soap alone also work.
- Spray in a well-ventilated workspace.
- Warn those who live with you about the stench. I don't want you kicked out of your home until my book about DIY houseboats is ready for you to spend money on.

To apply, either use the spray on stuff, or rub it on with a paper towel. Get every surface, even the insides. The better coated everything is, the more time you have to enjoy your boat before it rots.

How will this thing propel through water, you ask? Since I'm not a fan of paddling with bare palms, and since there is scrap wood around, let's build some paddles. This is as simple as it gets. Draw a paddle shape into some scrap plywood. Stick two scraps on top of each other and cut out two paddles.

This is also the part where you cut a notch into your wooden dowel, or whatever material you chose for a paddle rod.

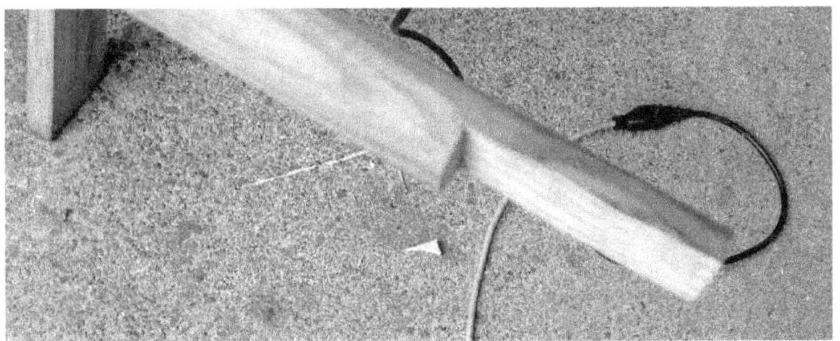

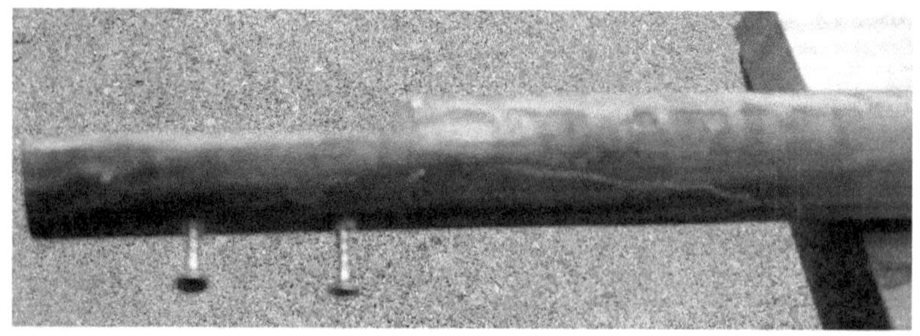

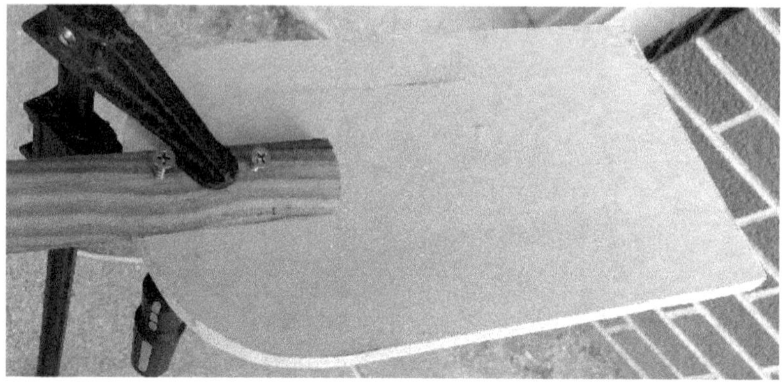

Paddle design is something you can play with. Paddles come in all shapes and sizes. Where proper boat hull design and careful gluing keep you safe out of the water, paddle design is a performance issue. The worst that happens, is you create an inefficient paddle, right?

Another item we might want is a name plate. I added this with a piece of scrap and a marker. Snowbank Lake, by the way, is beautiful lake in Minnesota's Boundary Waters. Visit it!

Next is something I worry about quite a lot when building boats: Will it fit into my SUV?

Easily! If you have a Sedan, this is light enough to strap down on the roof.

Look at a couple of things in the previous photo. First, the blue lifejacket is there. Wear a life jacket, whether you are a good swimmer or not. Second, that plastic sheeting protects the inside of my vehicle. Sort of. Finally, see that bag of bags behind the life jacket? That's my cell phone holder. It works. Take a gallon freezer bag. Fill it with crumpled paper or plastic bags and put your phone in it. You can tap through the freezer bag, the phone stays dry, and, if dropped overboard, it floats.

OK, bringing a phone takes away from the wonder of escaping to nature. I bring one, all the same. If there's cute duckling or a pretty sunset, the phone is a handy camera. Should my kids get in trouble, it's nice to be reachable. And I like having 9-1-1 at my fingertips if needed.

While we're thinking about transporting the boat, the plastic tarp is handy for keeping the tailgate clean, and more noticeably, not smelling like a lake.

Playing Around in the Water

We are about ready to go. One note, at the bottom of the cockpit, I have a sheet of 1/2" plywood to sit on. This distributes your weight across the bottom. A few 2x4's work, too. The back rim of the cockpit is kind of sharp, so consider placing an old pillow between that edge and your back.

And away we go. For your first trip, pick a small lake where you know the water is shallow. Stay close to shore. Tell people where you're going in case something bad happens.

Getting in the kayak take practice. If you've come with me this far, you should fit.

Once in the water, notice the splatter on the top cover. Paddling is a splashy business, with these paddles at least. All those splashes would be pooling up inside the boat if not for the cover.

Here I'm showing off some leg. Gotta market this book somehow. The other reason is to show you how the water is so close, and the vegetation is so close, that you feel like you are a part of the waterscape, not merely a visitor.

I like to fish. This boat is stable enough for fishing, and the cockpit leaves plenty of room for gear. You could consider building a little box on top of the cover to hold beverages and fishing gear. Make it waterproof against paddle splatter.

If you paddle with people who own 'professionally'
built kayaks, expect them to move much faster than
you. This kayak is not built for performance. A
longer, thinner kayak would be. I'd recommend
playing with designs.

And here is what could be the smile on your face
when you enjoy your own self-made fifty-dollar
kayak.

If you have ideas to share, please pop me a message
at my blog, ottosboatyard.wordpress.com.

Have fun and stay safe.
-Nate